sidewalk cruiseship

The Albuquerque Poet Laureate Series

Co-published with the City of Albuquerque's Department of Arts and Culture, the Albuquerque Poet Laureate Series features new and selected work by the city's Poet Laureate at the conclusion of their two-year term. Newly appointed poets will join Hakim Bellamy, Jessica Helen Lopez, Manuel González, Michelle Otero, and Mary Oishi as significant voices in the community who have been recognized with the honor of serving as the Poet Laureate and sharing their craft in the volumes published in the series.

Also available in the Albuquerque Poet Laureate Series:

Open-Hearted Horizon: An Albuquerque Poetry Anthology edited by Valerie Martínez and Shelle VanEtten de Sánchez

Commissions y Corridos: Poems by Hakim Bellamy

The Blood Poems by Jessica Helen Lopez

Bosque: Poems by Michelle Otero

Duende de Burque: Alburquerque Poems and Musings by Manuel González

SIDEWALK CRUISESHIP

mary oishi

University of New Mexico Press
Albuquerque

Printed in the United States of America

ISBN 978-0-8263-6623-8 (paper)
ISBN 978-0-8263-6624-5 (ePub)

Library of Congress Control Number: 2023917080

Founded in 1889, the University of New Mexico sits on the traditional homelands of the Pueblo of Sandia. The original peoples of New Mexico—Pueblo, Navajo, and Apache—since time immemorial have deep connections to the land and have made significant contributions to the broader community statewide. We honor the land itself and those who remain stewards of this land throughout the generations and also acknowledge our committed relationship to Indigenous peoples. We gratefully recognize our history.

Cover photographs by Isaac Morris and Wesley Tingey via Unsplash
Designed by Isaac Morris
Composed in Helvetica Neue and Minion Variable

For Sachi

Contents

1 | Galaxy Albuquerque

5 | tanka #1
7 | predawn sorority
8 | eight hundred feet, ten thousand years
10 | because shame
12 | sidewalk cruiseship
14 | high spark of low-heeled
15 | letter to myself before
16 | strength and mercy

19 | tanka #2
21 | ghost town
25 | pandemic notice
27 | John Prine in ICU
28 | we must stay apart
29 | bad news in a pandemic

33 | tanka #3
35 | self-care
37 | when i sing of seeds
39 | i beg your pardon
41 | today not one bird
42 | i swear plenty but
43 | Because Holidays

45 | tanka #4
47 | Albuquerque animals
49 | petals and rocks
50 | for Wanda Cooper-Jones
51 | dis-illusions
52 | prophesy

55 | tanka #5
57 | between children
58 | response to *Vairochana Teaching* (Patrick Nagatani)
60 | morning moon hanging
61 | it's Easter Eve but
62 | when we can hug again

65 | tanka #6
67 | One Song
68 | kind and distant / green and glass
72 | choice
73 | creation story retold
74 | taps for Afghanistan
75 | plea to a bomb

77 | tanka #7
79 | for Susan
80 | a place for sorrow
83 | desert life

85 | tanka #8
87 | Easter morning
88 | last visit
89 | diagnosis: syncope
91 | i thought i saw a monkey
92 | back to the present

85 | tanka #9
97 | the crone in my young vision
98 | lanterns in darkness

101 | Acknowledgments

Galaxy Albuquerque

Albuquerque gradually flicks on scattered stars
throughout neighborhoods: streetlights, porch lights,
while the rose halo of the powerful star
still graces the horizon

behind the lesser stars below:
queens of their kitchens,
abuelitas with their hands in corn flour

mothers worry about their daughters,
fathers feel proud of their children,
even those not theirs by blood

kids wish they were somewhere else
in a major galaxy like New York, Paris, LA,
others bask in the glow of their forever home

an old woman's glad for her new puppy
who circles her like the moon
she calls her Luna

another woman gets the news she will be
a grandmother for the first time, anticipates
the brightest star she'll ever see

approaching stars, receding stars,
passed out far from streetlights,
flickering cold

stars about to blink out
in sacred rooms with hushed tones
glistening eyes

each star holds storied mysteries,
celebrations behind dancing lights:
we can't begin to know them all

tourists in the windowed restaurant
at the top of Sandia Crest,
me in my stucco spaceship
docked in perfect position,
look out and take it in—
if the darkness holds pain
we can't see it—the
Galaxy of Albuquerque
sparkles across the night floor,
its collection of lights
our own Andromeda:
peaceful,
magnificent, a
comfortable fiction of stars

tanka #1

an elephant walks
into a flower bed with
no intent to harm
yet years of my care lie crushed
beneath oblivious feet

predawn sorority

i live by myself but not alone
woken by a mother's wail half a world away
her child buried in the rubble / in the well—she knows those shoes
i can't sleep
my dreams disturbed by a Mariupol grandma / troubled
her fleeing daughter and her babies may not make it to
the border

i'm troubled too
get up and worry / steep a pot of tea at 2:00 a.m.
sip slowly on hot tears   keep company with my sisters

pray that no more fall prey to brutality and madness
pray i myself stay loving / not fall prey to hate that maddens

slip my prayer past the missile trajectory to touch that one
who's on the brink
the sister underground
who tries to keep her cat and children calm
while inside trembling
to shore her up from my kindred heart
to let her know i have *picked up* the soundwaves of her suffering
to offer one small respite sipped from the quiet of my night
night by myself but not alone

eight hundred feet, ten thousand years

i center myself at Needle Rock,
rising eight hundred feet from the valley floor
the wind carries high elevation secrets
of elk herds, three or four big horn sheep,
a lone mountain lion

spirits of animals whose bones rest
on nearby Bone Mesa
dart under the sage at the base of the rock
growing from dust that eroded, blew around and settled
once the volcanic core hardened
all those millennia ago

tomorrow and ten thousand years past
gather here
where the earth once exploded new life
between mountain folds
the worries of now, my one small life,
are nothing after fifteen minutes here,
rolled down the slope,
carried away by the soft singing stream
at the very bottom of the canyon

while the dogs i brought
bound past me up and down
down and up and down again,
nothing to worry about:
no stalking ex can find me here,
beyond drama,
beyond time
bald eagle silent sailing,

holds ceremony above,
rabbits needlessly freeze under greenery by the trail,
dogs too free to bother chasing

i belong to this place
the wind can reveal its secrets—or not:
through the soles of my feet
on this sacred soil
i've already been told
absolutely everything
i need to know

because shame

because shame is the cell that multiplies, takes over,
spreads to places it does not belong, devours

because of words that never should be spoken
because of silent looks that blame louder than words

because the priest tells little girls *every time you think*
a bad thought, you drive another nail in Jesus's hands

because a mother tells her little son *big boys don't cry*
because the son puts on his mother's makeup

because the teacher calls him *faggot* in the classroom
when he's beat up, fights back, *he* gets suspended

because a woman tells her queer coming-out sister
you better not tell mom, it's gonna kill her

because parents disown their only daughter,
tell new friends *we don't have any children*

because the preacher says that he's against abortion
unless it can be proven that the baby's gay

because she's written out of daddy's will
for marrying a black man

because the thin one sneers *I would NEVER*
let myself go like that!

because of knives ground down in bone to needles,
leaving shame to fill like dirty water in the wounds

because track marks make us criminal, more shame—
street medicines numb only, never heal

because shame is hell on earth brought on by others' sin
most blasphemous: judge not! unless you're God, judge not

sidewalk cruiseship

it's just an old sofa
placed by the street
free for the taking
to make way for a newer
more up-to-date style:
it's trash

she's a Native woman
on the street a long time
it's a hard life
always moving
always vigilant
that stress wears you, you know?

park bench is hard metal
mission cot must be rented
by enduring righteous rebuke
promise of gold streets and mansions
from people who could
never do this
what she does every day, every day
out on the hot asphalt
all day long
they have no idea what it's like
when your feet ache
all the time
at the bottom
of much more gravity
than your own weight—

so beyond tired

suddenly life gifts her
a big round sofa
a sidewalk cruiseship:
she falls in, half laughing
legs up over the
fat sofa arm

feet floating, floating weightless
over the concrete sea

high spark of low-heeled

there she is, on the corner of Broadway and Lomas,
dancing,
wrapping her arms around herself,
throwing them open to the sky,
shouting commands to the drivers,
waiting   for the light to change

grand sweeping motions for them to go, go!
back to dancing,
wrapping her arms around herself,
throwing them open to the sky,
singing out the descriptors of her jumbled world
to the indifferent day
she's out of her mind, they think,
a fleeting dismissal
green light and they roll past,
glad their doors autolock

i miss the first light,
she makes no eye contact,
calls instead to the drifting cloud
that pays no mind on its way to the mountain

what trauma put her there,
incoherent on the corner?
what horrors made her
hold herself / abandon
hold herself / abandon
spinning out / back in like that?
what keeps her dancing,
embracing herself and reaching, reaching,
still sparking too high
to step off the curb?

letter to myself before

hang in there child
someday this pain
will feel like fairy tales
that happened to someone else
not you

after many tellings
it's just stories
from another incarnation
flat and harmless on the page
with faded illustrations
of someone you used to be
completely unrelated to you now
it's the joy of growing old
it's the life we claim
after we let go
let the past fall into fictions
resurrect ourselves brand new
into the now

hang in there child
someday this pain
will be a character
you once played

you'll barely remember
one-tenth of your lines
but those who said words that
helped you hang on
those you'll remember like
all-time favorite songs

strength and mercy

most times the mountain’s shaped like strength
i turn to it for refuge
but when the mountain lion lets me be
the mountain’s shaped like mercy—
me, like prayer

tanka #2

when we stay apart
quarantined in our lonely
it's when we realize
how tribal we are even
iPadded and iPhoned

ghost town

"dis town is coming like a ghost town"
was the song that kept singing
in an Albuquerque-adopted son's head
louder, and too loud,
for the silence downtown,
as he walked deserted streets,
past boarded-up windows

he took a few pictures:
a truck turning left
with no one in the crosswalk
(or the sidewalks either, for that matter)
except the son with a song in his head and
one unhoused man curled up
in his dirty blue blanket, in an alcove,
his few belongings nearby—
a water bottle and a backpack
in the corner, near his head,
already half ghost

one shop owner, windows intact,
has painted on them the face of
George Floyd
BLACK LIVES MATTER
#justiceforGeorgeFloyd
is the caption
it's more of a chant than a song,
but yeah,
i can see how your inside ears would sing
"dis town is coming like a ghost town"

another picture:
on the strip, one lone low rider,
red lights in the grille
a few blocks down, a chopper
all stretched out, yellow, chrome, and attitude

other than that, not much sign of life

Albuquerque's adopted son
is feeling deep despair

i doubt he ever took the Old Town Ghost Tour
back when things were open all the time
he wasn't a tourist
this is his home

who needs a ghost tour?
ghosts in every neighborhood,
hiding in the volcanoes,
ghosts everywhere

in the university ghetto,
an alcoholic, found three days later
in her backroom, dead
now she's refusing to leave,
lighting all the candles,
turning on the stereo at 3:00 a.m.
she's determined to get
somebody's attention

La Llorona? you'll have to ask
the ones born here about her

i can tell you, since i arrived,
one spirit runs down Zuni

looking for an unlocked car
to spend the night,
looking over her shoulder
for that one cop who
turned off his lapel camera
friends keep building her
memorials by the wall
at the trailer park
near where she went down,
before Zuni bends back to Central
they keep building over and over
but they keep being torn down
until they finally give up

this ghost, not on the Old Town Ghost Tour—
too far removed

nor the ghost with the black gloves,
los guantes negros, holding a shovel,
wishing he had answered his
daughter's calls so that
no wellness-turned-death call
had followed

nor is the ghost on a hill
near the manicured neighbors
just under the mountain,
the ones with the mag*nifi*cent
westward views
he wasn't well, he wasn't to be
reasoned with, he didn't belong there,
so the cops were called
"dis town is coming like a ghost town"
yes, it's a ghost town
spirits that go back more than three hundred years,

long before this country
ever breathed its name

didn’t you see that sign
on your last picture?
it says,
SOME TEARS BECOME FLAMES

don’t despair, son,
that’s Albuquerque talking
and she damn well knows
what she’s talking about.

pandemic notice

i notice how stay-at-home can be
house arrest or fortress,
depending on my focus

i notice how pets, once
amusement and responsibilities,
become eyes i can look into,
not on a screen, but within inches,
how they are living warmth
i can touch and hold

i notice when somebody else shops for me
they don't care about the amount of green
on the bananas, or the furthest out
expiration date on the cereal

i notice when they hurry away from
dropping the bags on my porch,
hustling to pay the rent,
taking risks for those of us
who can't afford to and
can afford *not* to,
that i am grateful, green bananas and all

i notice maskless people
walking down the sidewalk
in front of my house
i notice those who wear their masks
over their mouth with their nose exposed—
i marvel at how little some understand
the purpose of things

i notice songbirds
when they're in the tree,
i notice when they're gone—
and it's a worry

i notice, with invisible danger
lurking who knows where,
i want to be told as much truth
as anyone knows:
the sleuths, the scientists,
those who can realistically tell me
how to keep myself safe:
i have no interest in comfortable lies
that could sneak the enemy
past my door

i notice that i miss ritual and
shared traditions so much
i hung Christmas lights for the first time,
sometimes let them burn all day

i notice what i miss the most
and what i look forward to
are the same

i notice, even at my age,
i can form new habits
i can adapt
i can learn
i can change

John Prine in ICU

not one familiar voice,
not one familiar touch, only
masked strangers, the
shum-shum-BAH
shum-shum-BAH
of the ventilator
trying to breathe when
you can't

this is no way
for a poet to die

we must stay apart

we must stay apart
now when we need each other
most, shelves bare of touch

bad news in a pandemic

it's the kind of news
you want to tell a friend in person,
hand on their hand,
eyes brim full so they already know
what you're about to say
is going to feel like drowning,
but they know you won't
let them go under—
that's why you're here

when the news
must go by phone,
like morse code,
flashed from a boat
far from the shore,
through morning fog,
hesitant—
coming through in hints
until it's fully received,
pieced together,
the fog lifts

then the silence   the long   silence

can't see, but fear your friend is drowning

are you okay?

no, i'm not okay!
then the torrent: theirs and yours

this is not the way to deliver bad news:
in separate squalls,

each trying not to succumb

tanka #3

tick tick tick the dogs
are sleeping oh why did i
say you could skip tonight's call
in this cave one hundred years
like i'm the last one breathing

self-care

tried to think of a way to save it—
maybe i could remove the clear plastic,
clean underneath? but no

mold was embedded in the dust jacket
even if i could clean it outside,
moisture, mold made the pages
wavy brown, pungent,
a sacrilege of black and white
illustrations, photographs distorted:
how to arrange flowers,
written by a Japanese expert—
i was certain i could learn something,
some mystical aesthetic principle
that would delight me like new tea

but my throat was starting to seize
just like in that sick building

sudden swift decision:

step on the toe release
up, the trash lid
in, the book!
disease and intrigue
tied up quickly with
empty olive jar,
dog food bag,
wadded up paper towels,
dryer lint

even ikebana corrupted
gets sent to the curb,
life too delicate to save
any more carriers

when i sing of seeds

when i sing of seeds
mine is not a song of acorns and grains,
kernels and cones,
not when i sing of seeds

when i sing of seeds
falling from trees,
wrapped in fruit,
floating lightly bearded in the breeze,
in a bird's beak, a squirrel's cheek,
a gardener's loving hand

i sing not of seeds but of
blossoms fragrant,
bursting fuchsia and crimson and gold
i sing of majestic trees
that join wind and earth and sun
for two thousand years
when i sing of seeds

when i sing of seeds i sing
harvest, sing baskets of corn to be husked,
sing peas to be shelled, shells to be cracked
and released of their nutmeats
when i sing of seeds

when i sing of seeds i sing
roasting and baking and grilling,
sing conversations around the table,
silverware clanking, appetites satisfied
when i sing of seeds

when i sing of seeds i sing
thirty years down the road,
a child yet unborn crunching into an apple
when i sing of seeds i sing of
bouquets picked and handed to
mothers with love in the year 2999

when i sing of seeds
my song rises
verse after verse into
all that is life,
a swell of possibility
when i sing of seeds

when i sing of seeds
i sing down seven generations
times seven times seven
when i sing of seeds
my song never ends
my song never ends when i sing of seeds

i beg your pardon

i beg your pardon for Leonard Peltier
i beg your pardon for Mumia Abu-Jamal
i beg your pardon for Crystal Mason

i beg your pardon for the nine percent on death row
wrongfully accused,
dubiously judged, not by a jury of their peers

i beg your pardon for all those imprisoned
instead of treated for their trauma
for the resulting addictions

i beg your pardon for all those who never had a chance,
those you barely educated,
barely doctored,
refused to hire   refused to pay a living wage,
drove to the black market, drove to needles of despair

i beg your pardon   not your pity   but
owning up to the part you played

until you make it right:

pardon me, but i do not pardon you for
letting the wall street robbers rob us all, scot-free
pardon me, but i do not pardon you for
demanding our tax money while billionaires
spend their share amusing themselves in a
high-flying phallus
for a few minutes' joyride here and there

pardon me, but i do not pardon you for
sparing joe arpaio from taking the smallest dose
of his own medicine

pardon me, but i do not pardon you
for the bundys who owed millions, then
met federal agents with rifles rather than pay,
who occupied a federal facility more heavily armed
than AIM when they occupied Alcatraz or Wounded Knee

pardon me if i'd rather comfort the mothers of
Anthony Huber
Joseph Rosenbaum
Gaige Grosskreutz
than give kyle a tissue for his tears

i beg your pardon for interrupting your smirking reverie
but i'm not sorry that i see you for
exactly who you are: with whip and noose,
ammo and gun, all the keys on a big cold loop
on your tight ass belt

how can i grant pardon
to you, who pardons all the bullies
if they ever get charged at all,
who steals the lives of all under your boot, under your knee,
who act like we're your big game prey,
posing for selfies with us, grinning that big proud grin

today not one bird

today not one bird
thin snow caps on ev'rything
the hush before war

i swear plenty but

i won't drop the f-bomb in
my poem just to
shock the stereotype of
Asian women out of you

Because Holidays

Because sun sinks too early in winter.
Because light disappears from your eyes.

Because this year it's brown and bare branches.
Because snow glare is so worth the shielding.
Because spring melts to rivers to quench us.

Because there are seasons we won't ever see.
Because we grow fixed. We go frozen.

Because we need this day.
Because there is no forever.
Because change. Because change.

Because light comes around.
Because light follows darkness.

Because holidays. Because holy days.
Because hope. Because hope.

tanka #4

i don’t do extras
the builder explains dragging
the stone lantern
to my gate *but i am a man*
who loves to create beauty

Albuquerque animals

Bosque porcupine
sleeps high in the crook of the cottonwood tree
ducks at their pit stop,
an island in the drought-drawn Rio Grande

prairie dogs on Kirtland,
adjacent to the dog park,
chattering their excited warning
of the coyote loping along
past the colony

roadrunner
that mortally wounds the dove
whose partner mourns for three days,
sending his grief out for blocks
not for pity
but because
if he held it in
he would be too heavy to fly

thin-eyed poet
in her pandemic cave
at the base of the giant mulberry
with her two canine pals,
speaking her new poem over and over aloud,
as is the thin-eyed poet's peculiar ritual

curious hummingbird
drawn to the poet's window
as if her words were morning glories,
certain such nectar

could sustain his beating wings
if only he could take it in

sandhill cranes
finding the corn that fell
in Los Poblanos Fields Open Space,
blessing the earth with their gray angel landings,
blessing the breeze with ethereal calls

petals and rocks

until she's blistered
until her hands bleed

a mother will pluck the flower
from every stem
shake the blossoms
from every blooming tree
lie down herself
if that's what it takes
to cushion the path
her child walks

still they will choose
to climb the rock wall

for Wanda Cooper-Jones

mother of Ahmaud Arbery

mother who never
wanted this mountain to climb
holds the scene of him
first time in her arms   and climbs
until merrick garland cries

dis-illusions

i met you before
i know i did, i—
or was i dreaming?

perfect harmony
in song is not the same as
by the breakfast nook

it was not the song
that made me remember love
it was the static

i saw lightning where
there was no lightning, love
where there was no love

love is a great drug
but the hangover has a
mortality rate

prophesy

a Diné poet/mother/multimedia artist told me today
that, according to the indigenous calendar,
we're about to leave what she calls "hell" cycles,
enter the cycles she and her people call "heaven,"
when the Pleiades is directly overhead.

"It will get worse before it gets better
but by 2038 the mixed people—and look at us,
we're all mixed—

the mixed people will take us back to
living with the earth again.

So says the prophesy," she said,
smiling down at her boy.

So says the prophesy, re-beats my weary heart,
weary of the cycles of pandemic hell, of
conspiracy hell, of
mass shootings hell, of
history-erasing hell,
hell after hell—but
So says the prophesy.

So says the prophesy carries me like a refrain,
glowing, warming my winter heart,
waiting for the mixed grandchild
who will bring heaven to earth for me this year
no matter where the Pleiades appears
on the night of her birth

perhaps she *will* help take us back,
perhaps by 2038 she and all the mixed peoples of earth
will usher in the “heaven” cycles.   at least—

So says the prophesy.

who am i to disbelieve?

tanka #5

from your nest of souls
fly to the one whose heartbeat
is your nine-month drum
we are waiting here with hope
your song and another nest

between children

another Easter
this year i didn't even hard-boil
let alone paint some eggs

maybe when the little one is here
and old enough, i will smile as i go through the
checkout line with all the colors, special swirls,
cardboard circle stands that make the eggs
look like heads of fairies, sailors, boys in suits—
in the box with crayons,
little wire holders for dipping

i remember those days
when my girl was little, the crafts we did:
Easter eggs, baked clay jewelry, model cars—

without a child, life has less magic,
we almost forget how to play

response to *Vairochana Teaching* (Patrick Nagatani)

truth veiled in fiction
becomes again truth
Vairochana, on his lotus,
masked by the veil between
magic and what we call real,
extends his hand,
invites connection,
invites a visitation to the dream:
nonviolence, forgiveness wisdom,
invites investigation of
cultures seldom noticed
in the midst of a
three-culture myth,
glimpses of orange-robed monks
near the red-roofed temple,
by the taco truck,
Tibetan phrases overheard
(but not identified as such)
in the checkout line

Asians, like barely visible shadows,
move among us

come behind the veil, he invites,
behind the split curtain between
kitchen and restaurant dining room,
behind the walls where no English,
or Spanish, or Tewa are spoken
by those who took refuge in the high desert
after jungle wars,

who cut hair and paint nails so
their children have a chance,
so they can send some back
to those left behind

come behind the veil and see
those whose ancestors came here
generations ago: farmed, opened stores,
won medals in war

whose children and grandchildren
now teach at every level, now heal:
practice medicine, open health clinics,
practice law, preside as judges,
run nonprofits, do community organizing,
make art, make music, write poetry

truth sits behind the mask, truth stands in front
come closer, look with both eyes,
see—and see

morning moon hanging

morning moon hanging
in a periwinkle sky
last night's dream fading

it's Easter Eve but

if tomorrow were Christmas,
the only thing i'd want
is to see your face,
to hold you to my chest
so you could feel the comfort of
where you always belong

if tomorrow were Christmas,
it wouldn't matter that
i had no time for shopping
(much as i love to give
the humblest of presents
sought out with love)
if all i can give you
is a shaft of light
brought back from a hole
found near the end of the tunnel,
then i give it with hope
that this is the long dark
underground passage
to the bright world we dreamed of
where humans come together
as one family, connected,
revering our Mother,
protecting our siblings
in their feathers, scales, and fur
where we value what has value:
loved ones, art, community
where the rush is not to grab it,
but to cherish what we have
and to
honor who we are

when we can hug again

when we can hug again
you're going to feel
a little bit warmer
i'm going to hold on
just a few seconds more

tanka #6

say it isn't so
my daughter is forty now
just week before last
she was eighteen and travelin'
week after next she'll be me

One Song

after Li-Young Lee's "One Heart"

Look at the stage. Even music
is born

out of silence. The first note
is inside you, forming

at either end of choking.
The work of voice
was always courage, coaxing
one song from every shivering thing.

kind and distant / green and glass

was this a dream of unfamiliar birdsongs
cloud-haloed mountains
of pagoda-pierced cityscapes
pachinko and neon
five-story tv screens
five-way crosswalks thronging at two o'clock
tuesday afternoon

was it a dream of forty-foot bronze buddhas
of fuzzy-antlered buck bowing to
yellow-capped school children
of westerners waiting like hunters with cameras
for geisha to emerge for
a fleeting twenty seconds
on a Kyoto street

was it a dream of glimmers of great grandparents
given names a few dates
at long last

was it a dream of artfully prepared foods
of a kind old Japanese couple
elegant and loving
hosting us in their home
was it a dream of narrow
Yamanashi alleys
and bicycle bells
of sunsets on rice fields
sunsets on rivers
dotted with cranes and lovers

was it a dream of high-speed trains
with ample legroom
filled with men in suits reading
comic books newspapers and porn
was it a dream of gourmet bento lunches
in train stations
ubiquitous vending machines
with peace and hope cigarettes
canned lattes and fresh cucumbers

was it a dream of upper middle-class women
and their well-groomed children
wearing shirts with nonsensical
English sayings:

> crack
> if the sky (or heaven) falls
> we will catch (the lark)
> of twinkle stars
>
> lily poem
> casual dog style
>
> string along with organizer
>
> don't come home alone
> when darkening
>
> i want to see the change in the world
> with this eye

engrish engrish everywhere
made me wonder what those kanji shirts
and tattoos at home *really* say?

ninety-eight-dollar shirts at the mall
twenty-three-dollar chopsticks
curtained photo booths
packed with young girls
eager to put their faces
in a field of cartoon flowers
or sparkling stars
then draw or write and decorate
all over the shot to create
stamp-sized works of pop art
they will save and trade

was this a dream of a kabuki actor
in a grand white and gold kimono
floating across a Tokyo stage
of the Kodo troupe of taiko drummers
and rivers of blue silk
enhancing his performance
was it a dream of
a series of nine escalators
going up and up and up
in a Kyoto rail station
twenty-first century echo
of the steep seven stone flights
to enlightenment at the
eighth century Minobu temple

this morning, my last morning in Japan
it feels like i am about to wake
from a strange and beautiful dream
a dream from deep in my
subconscious
disciplined and chaotic
ancient and high tech

kind and distant
green and glass
mystic and corporate
now with ancestral memory
revived contemporary
i must return to my daily life
in America, my mother's adopted
post-war home
where she made sure life would go on
just as they have done
in the land she left behind
where they have outlasted
every nightmare
where they have steadfastly refused
to give up
just like her
just like me

choice

every birthing mother
rides with death for a while—
some for a few minutes,
some hours, some days
some all the way past the point
where they can wrap new life in their arms,
leap from his chariot,
or even themselves dismount alone

who dares to force her stay aboard
no matter how child she is, how old,
no matter how she got there:
father, grandpa, violent stranger—
even if it's *guaranteed*
he'll drive her past the veil?

creation story retold

response to Birth Garment 1: Pregnant Amazon *(Judy Chicago)*

she arose carrying
millions of potential daughters,
yet from under her rib
she grew Adam, a son

he came into the world
covered in her blood and fluids,
grown in—and of—her natural body,
the milk of her growing him still

now that he nestles in her arms,
safe and loved,
he dares to say
she came from *him*

she overlooks this foolishness,
gives him what he needs,
generation after generation

someday, she hopes, he will
look in her face,
really see her
while there's still time,
before his hubris
destroys everything

taps for Afghanistan

taps play for the boy who
left the recruiting station,
fists full of promises,
invincibly young,
so sure he would
come back alive,
collect the benefits

but some roadside bomb,
some helicopter crash,
some "ally" that he trained,
secretly bitter,
seeking revenge,
maybe even friendly fire—
the truth is rarely told

now a lone trumpet mourns
its slow and piercing witness:
a life was lost,
cut short so soon

the saddest thing:
nobody even knows
the reason why

plea to a bomb

please, bomb, miss all the
mothers about to give birth,
miss all the babies—
if you're a smart bomb you'll dive,
explode in a field somewhere

tanka #7

what is a dream where
ghosts living and dead come to
shake up settled ground
nobody loved is ever
buried or buried for long

for Susan

didn't make headlines
cameras weren't rolling
earth didn't shift, rivers didn't rise
no Geiger counters moved
no seismographs

stock market didn't tick up
or down as a result
not a penny was spent or made
bookies didn't cash in
gamblers didn't cash out

pundits didn't comment
politicians didn't weigh in
scholars didn't write papers
pollsters didn't call

heck, the barmaid didn't even notice

but oh the joy! the smile
that spread across her face
when after twenty years
she danced

a place for sorrow

when my friend Jo goes out
she puts her sorrow in a kitchen drawer
between the vegetable peeler and the spatulas
covers it with a bright red-hot pad
to keep it warm and comforted while she's away
don't worry, she tells her sorrow,
i'll be back to keep you company
but i can't take you with me
out into the world—not out there
i've got volunteer work to do
political causes, research at the university

while she's gone
she won't think back all those years
to the night the police officer
shows up at her door at midnight
she knows him, Shawn, he's in her night class
at the university
she's happy to see him—
they don't get much company these days at any hour
her son is never in trouble
such a good boy
she knows this must be a friendly visit
while Shawn is on patrol
she invites him into the living room
is your husband here, he asks
oh, such a gentleman, she thinks
can you get him?
oh, he really wants to meet bill, okay

drunk driver . . . so sorry . . . your son . . .
gone . . . gone . . . gone . . .

that's what Shawn comes to say at midnight?

but . . . but . . . he just graduated college . . .
his fiancée . . . such a lovely girl . . .

she asks, expressionless, do you want a cup of tea?

now from the kitchen drawer her sorrow beckons
but she gently reassures it on her way out the door
i won't leave you very long
her psychiatrist friend says
why don't you flush it down the commode
oh no, she says, then it might go bother someone else
and this is *my* sorrow
i've got shoulders to carry it
and i've got the perfect place to keep it
while i'm gone

Jo rarely leaves the house
now that she's a fourscore widow
that old sorrow's getting more insistent every day
so she invites others in for tea and conversation
and speaks of healthcare policy
of obscure history from her native Spain
of today's headlines, two police officers gunned down
in the line of duty
of Gloria Steinem's refrigerator
sparsed with only scotch and ice cream
of her late husband's woodcuts
done in Taos where light is grand
of her poor proud students who
would never think of buying day-old bread
of Greenwich Village back when you could walk at night
of happier days when her son made that sugar bowl
from two small jars

she recalls the hippies with a smile
groove on it, that's what they used to say

and all the while her old companion drapes her shoulders
brooding, brooding straight at you, and
you can never quite spend time with Jo alone

desert life

rare indeed in the desert
to fall asleep to the sound of rain,
each drop a soft note of comfort

rarer still to wake up to rain as well,
the steady drizzle a quiet insistent anthem
for us to go on

tanka #8

leaves not meant to fall
before the autumn dries them
drains them of their green
were you always golden then
to have left without a word

for Janice Mirikitani (1941–2021)

Easter morning

told my dad some good news
last night on the phone

he gave me that "Hey HEY"
congratulating laugh he always does

it was so good to hear
his voice his laugh again

even if it was only in a dream

last visit

there was a window:
she looked in that direction but
she didn't see

she didn't see the trees
at the end of her yard
she didn't see the birds
singing in them
she didn't see the pleasant
summer sky with the faraway clouds

all she could see
was five years of memories
her granddaughter waving
not knowing it was goodbye

diagnosis: syncope

it happens suddenly—
the brain deprived of oxygen
you're all up in the
overwhelming feeling of going down
of blacking out
nothing else matters
sound of your own breath
making you feel worse:
there are no bills due
no gossip juicy enough
to have audience with
a mind that's fading
that's facing death

you realize you don't
get to pick the moment:
could be at a dinner party
or in line at the store
in the middle of a
conversation with an old friend
or a new
anywhere
any time
you don't get to pick—
it just happens

surreal in that emergency room
when they just ignore you
"stand over there
we'll get to you—
it just got busy
all of a sudden"

all of a sudden
the world is blinking
nothing else matters
reduced to the mercy
of paid angels
pacing themselves calmly between
all of a sudden bullets
all of a sudden stab wounds
all of a sudden consciousness
blinking out on the world

i thought i saw a monkey

i thought i saw a monkey
standing on the sidewalk
dirty jeans a size too big
hanging low on his hips

i thought my new glasses
would help me to see right
but as i got closer
to my great surprise
there was no monkey at all
just an old fire hydrant paint peeling
with some cast iron showing through
in random rusty patterns
that i saw {primate}

how can i trust these eyes that
age and atrophy
just when my inner vision's
slowly growing wise

back to the present

an old envelope
that familiar handwriting
time thieves but leaves this

alabaster vase
i remember sweet and soft
and white gardenias

wind makes that strange sound
i wonder if i
will grow old alone

tanka #9

there is a time when
the old writer falls asleep
pen still in drooped hand
falling in a wordless line
off the page into darkness

the crone in my young vision

to my surprise was me.
her presence alone
commanded respect.
nothing less. and

she had no regrets.

oh, she had made mistakes
but they turned out to be
some of her best teachers.

how can I ever become her?
i cried, broken.
i'm as far from her
as a worm from the moon!

and i was.

square your shoulders,
was all she said.

i'm decades rising,
three words pulling the tides.

lanterns in darkness

lanterns in darkness
quiet spirits floating down
the river as light

sidewalk cruiseship

Acknowledgments

Many thanks to the poets who consistently encouraged and supported my work in recent years, including: Margaret Randall, Sandy Yannone, Richard Vargas, Dodici Azpadu, and in memoriam, Gary Brower.

Additional thanks to those who preceded me as Albuquerque Poet Laureate: Hakim Bellamy, Jessica Helen Lopez, Manuel Gonzales, and Michelle Otero, each of whom elevated poetry and represented Albuquerque, "the City of Poets," admirably.

Finally, a word of appreciation for those who served on the Albuquerque Poet Laureate Committee, for their work behind the scenes during my tenure: Don McIver, Mindy Grossberg, Liza Wolff Francis, Valerie Martinez, and Tanesia Hale-Jones.

And to the following publications, websites, artists, and projects for their original publication of and/or inspiration for individual poems in this volume, sometimes published in a slightly different form:

Open-Hearted Horizon: An Albuquerque Poetry Anthology (2024): "Albuquerque animals," "Galaxy Albuquerque," and "prophesy" (published as "prophesy on an Albuquerque day")

New Mexico Poetry Anthology (2023): "ghost town"

Dear Future Self: ArtWorks Student Art & Poetry Anthology 2022–2023: "pandemic notice"

Bombfire (bombfirelit.com) (2021): "for Susan" and "last visit"

Fixed and Free Poetry Anthology 2021: "Easter morning," "eight hundred feet, ten thousand years" (published as "800 feet, ten thousand years"), and "strength and mercy"

The Blue Nib (2020): "John Prine in ICU"

Fixed and Free Poetry Anthology 2018: "diagnosis: syncope" and "the crone in my young vision"

"back to the present" (last stanza only) was published in *2023 Poets' Picnic: A Celebration of Nature, Calligraphy, Music & Poetry*, a limited edition chapbook "plea to a bomb" was published as a broadsheet in "Pressing Letters," a collaborative art project funded by the Fulcrum Fund, 2023

"Because Holidays" was performed at Mayor Tim Keller's inauguration, January 1, 2022

"today not one bird" was published on miriamswell.wordpress.com, 2022

"creation story retold" was written in response to *Birth Garment 1: Pregnant Amazon* by Judy Chicago in the permanent collection of the Albuquerque Museum

"response to *Vairochana Teaching* (Patrick Nagatani)" was written in response to *Vairochana Teaching* by Patrick Nagatani in the permanent collection of the Albuquerque Museum